Developing
a Culture
for Diversity
in a week

CHRIS SPEECHLEY
AND RUTH WHEATLEY

Hodder & Stoughton

HODDER HEADLINE GROUP

The Institute of Management (IM) is the leading
organisation for professional management. Its purpose is
to promote the art and science of management in every
sector and at every level, through research, education,
training and development, and representation of
members' views on management issues.
This series is commissioned by IM Enterprises Limited,
a subsidiary of the Institute of Management, providing
commercial services.

**Management House,
Cottingham Road,
Corby,
Northants NN17 1TT
Tel: 01536 204222;
Fax: 01536 201651
Website: http://www.inst-mgt.org.uk**

Registered in England no 3834492
Registered office: 2 Savoy Court, Strand,
London WC2R 0EZ

Orders: please contact Bookpoint Ltd, 39 Milton Park, Abingdon, Oxon OX14 4TD.
Telephone: (44) 01235 400414, Fax: (44) 01235 400454. Lines are open from 9.00–6.00,
Monday to Saturday, with a 24 hour message answering service.
Email address: orders@bookpoint.co.uk

British Library Cataloguing in Publication Data
A catalogue record for this title is available from The British Library

ISBN 0 340 781718

First published	2001
Impression number	10 9 8 7 6 5 4 3 2 1
Year	2004 2003 2002 2001

Cover photograph from Telegraph Colour Library.

Typeset by SX Composing DTP, Rayleigh, Essex.
Printed in Great Britain for Hodder & Stoughton Educational, a division of Hodder
Headline Plc, 338 Euston Road, London NW1 3BH by Cox & Wyman Ltd, Reading,
Berkshire.

CONTENTS

Diversity, a word which originally meant simply variety, has
come to be used as a specialised term to describe a workplace
that includes people from various backgrounds and cultures.
It is understood here as involving a managerial approach that:

- seeks first and foremost to treat people as
  individuals
- acknowledges the special circumstances or
  particular context that may lead to exclusion for
  some groups of people
- works to change that situation
- develops a workforce within which people are valued
  for the contribution they make.

Both at home and on the international scale, the ability to
manage across different cultures has become an essential
business skill. Successfully creating a corporate culture for
diversity, however, involves wholesale change at individual
and organisational levels of management. An approach that
can achieve such change will be explained and described over
the coming week. It is centred on cultural development and
change, and:

i) emphasises inclusiveness, openness and fairness
ii) offers a positive outlook on the many differences, as well
    as the similarities, between us all; and
iii) presents a developmental training process, known as
    Multi-Dimensional Training (MDT), that has been found
    effective in various contexts, including diversity-related
    projects.

Our plans for the week are to:

- define what we mean by diversity and explore its potential benefits for people and business
- place diversity in context as a theoretical subject and look at the effects of discrimination on some minority groups
- introduce the four phases of our approach to developing a culture for diversity
- look at changing the organisational 'hardware' – systems, policies and processes – to support cultural change
- move into the more difficult 'software' side of change – people and culture
- develop our understanding of the theories and techniques underlying Multi-Dimensional Training (MDT)
- outline the 'building blocks' for an MDT programme.

Developing a Culture for Diversity in a week will provide a guide to helping individuals, teams and organisations to work together in a way that ensures:

- people are valued
- people are helped to contribute and feel a part of their organisation
- people are able to develop and learn within an inclusive workplace context
- an organisation gains maximum benefits from a successful, open culture.

Our main emphasis will be on achieving a culture for diversity that is also a culture for good practice and high performance.

What is diversity?

After briefly considering the changes in western society that have created a need for managing diversity in the workplace, today we will begin to focus on:

- the features of an organisation that welcomes diversity
- our heritage of bureacratic organisation and its effects on management and corporate culture.

The business case for managing diversity will be considered and illustrated, and we will attempt to briefly describe how a culture for diversity might look and feel.

Our changing social context

The need for better integration at work reflects a changing population profile in western society and in the workforce itself. Most western industrial workplaces, except in times of war, were largely managed by men, until very recently, and these men were usually white. This situation has now changed and continues to change. In the United States, it is now predicted that white males themselves will soon be in a minority as new entrants to the workforce.

Many more women have now joined the workforce and achieved responsible positions, while ethnic groups in employment have also increased. However, there is still evidence of inequalities affecting these groups.

Unemployment levels within black or ethnic minority groups are higher than for whites. In management, as in all the main professions, the proportion of black, ethnic and female workers who reach senior levels remains low.

Factors that work to exclude those groups of people who most obviously differ from the traditional norm can also work to exclude other groups and individuals, who may differ from the organisational norm.

Many companies now consciously aim to recruit a higher proportion of people outside the old norms, but their efforts rarely translate into equal success for targeted groups. Poor retention of, and comparatively limited career progress for, minority groups are still problems in many organisations.

In the United States, where positive discrimination favouring protected minorities has been practised for many years, their success is still relatively limited. Positive discrimination can itself cause problems, in that those outside targeted groups often resent and may undermine resulting career advances.

Most importantly, even within the litigation-prone United States, positive discrimination seems not to have stopped harassment and discrimination against protected groups.

Managing diversity well means involving everyone in promoting integration and cohesion, rather than division. To achieve this, we need to understand how diversity management can benefit everyone, not just minorities.

Developing a diverse culture is about:

- seeing others as individuals
- valuing the skills and abilities they bring to an organisation
- not seeing people first and foremost in terms of their membership of a particular group.

This approach has far-reaching implications leading to strategies that will differ from those of an equal opportunities perspective. For example, within the context of a diversity approach, it would be recognised that some individuals from some groups need particular training (such as assertiveness) or development experience (such as a managerial course). But special training would not routinely be provided for everyone in a group, as within an equal opportunities context; instead there would be an attempt to discriminate on a needs basis.

Diversity within organisations

A business within which diversity is accepted and welcomed would look feature, at every level:

- openness – rejection of secrecy as a way of managing
- understanding – a will to enquire about and explore issues before judging or evaluating them
- honesty – an acceptance of the need to deal in the truth, even where the truth is not pleasant
- fearlessness – a safe environment in which people have the confidence to say what they really think or feel
- learning – an acceptance of the need for everyone to move forward and develop through experience, exploration and learning
- responsibility – a willingness on everyone's part to take responsibility for the way the organisation is, rather than blame others for culture-linked problems
- highly developed communications – a readiness to work on continuous information sharing and high-quality interactions
- a lack of knee-jerk blame – a will to explore the reasons for mistakes or failures and to learn from them.

Such a culture would be a platform for diversity, with an inclusive approach assuming importance as a core value and way of life, rather than as a goal to be aimed for.

The legacy of bureaucracy

In most organisations, however, we have to contend with a different reality to that described above. An organisation is made up of individuals who usually work at different levels and hold varying degrees of responsibility and power. For understandable, historic reasons, most organisations are structured as hierarchies.

The bureaucratic, hierarchical organisation is becoming

Max Weber: bureaucracy and rationalisation

At the opening of the twentieth century, Weber described a rational–legal authority system – a bureaucracy – in which authority was exercised by a system of rules and procedures through the offices that people held.

A bureaucratic organisation was structured around official functions bound by rules. These functions were, in turn, structured into administrative offices organised into a hierarchy and separated from the ownership of the means of production.

Weber thought bureaucracy was the most technically efficient form of organisation for his time, but bureaucracies have been criticised from at least the 1950s for stifling inspiration and creativity. Since the 1970s, the term bureaucracy has acquired overtones of inefficiency and bureaucratic organisations are usually characterised as dinosaurs, weighed down with red tape. Most large, bureaucratic organisations have been subject to downsizing from the 1980s, as a flatter structure is now favoured to enable greater organisational flexibility and responsiveness.

---

scarce as we begin a new century, but it is proving difficult to break the mould of control-based management thinking and practice. We still seem to find it hard not to think of organisations as machines, directed from the executive level, by various levers and drivers. This emphasis on systems and control tends to neglect the human aspect of organisations.

If we think about it, we know that organisations are really

complex communities, with all the human problems that follow. Yet the metaphor of the mechanistic view is almost built into our existing management thinking. This has far-reaching consequences for our ability to create cultures that can encompass a diverse workforce.

The mechanistic view of organisations, into which most of us are likely to slip, undermines our chances of achieving the organisational qualities – openness, honesty, responsibility and lack of fear – that are needed in a culture for diversity.

A few organisations have successfully developed a culture for diversity and demonstrated the business benefits that can be achieved. The value of a strategic approach to 'diversity' in terms of fairness and performance management is recognised as having the potential to make management more effective in general and to achieve a representative staff profile.

Some British retailers, including B&Q and Littlewoods, now recognise both the business and the social importance of achieving greater diversity. These companies have made diversity central and try to ensure, through their policies and processes, that it is achieved in practice.

The business case for seeking to manage people in a fair and inclusive way rests strongly on the following issues:

- *Staff retention* – some practitioners claim significant benefits in lower recruitment and training costs.
- *Broadened customer base* – by drawing in and retaining a wider spectrum of people as employees, a broader section of customers can also be attracted and retained.

Case study: diversity at Allstate Insurance Co, Illinois

Diversity is integral to strategy for Allstate Insurance. The company develops goals, leadership responsibility and rewards to foster diversity, and aims to employ a diverse workforce to improve business results.
Both the customer base and customer satisfaction levels have increased since this approach was implemented and Allstate has linked these increases to aspects of diversity management. Through employing, involving and closely managing the careers of people from many different backgrounds, Allstate became a leader in United States insurance for several market sectors, including Hispanics, African-Americans, retired people and working mothers.
Strategic diversity management for Allstate involves:
- board level participation, responsibility and accountability on diversity issues
- links to business plans and benefits at all levels
- employee ownership of diversity objectives
- commitment of resources for training and research
- a pro-active, approach to diversity through recruitment, marketing and supplier selection
- building diversity considerations into performance and reward systems.

Source: 'Diversity at Allstate: a competitive weapon' by Louisa Wah, *Management Review*, July/August 1999, pp24–30.

- *Broader understanding of customer needs* – staff from different backgrounds can help the organisation to better cater for the needs of their communities.
- *An open, more adaptive culture* – by focusing on people's performance and development on the basis of competence rather than group membership, an organisation will

---

Case study: diversity at DuPont

A United States-based multicultural team at DuPont gained around $45 million in new business by changing the way decorating materials are developed and marketed. The changes included new colours that team members knew, from their experience within other cultures, would appeal more to their overseas customers.

Case study: diversity at Lloyds TSB

For Lloyds TSB, the business case for increasing diversity is extremely important and the forging of more links between the bank and local communities is known to have had bottom-line effects. At one branch in an area with a large Bangladeshi community, for example, the recruitment of more representative staff from the local population increased sales of pensions and other financial products by approximately 30 to 40 per cent in six months.
Source: 'Improving recruitment and promotion opportunities for ethnic minorities', *Equal Opportunities Review*, No 85, May/June 1999, pp15–20.

usually become more vibrant and competitive.
- *Greater innovation* – knowledge and ideas are more easily developed as people communicate more. This is especially important for multi-cultural and multi-functional teams.
- *A more committed workforce* – people who are valued and listened to will usually become more committed to their employer, and much evidence now suggests that this links to better business performance.

Feeling alive – the benefits of an open culture

The openness that is key to a culture for diversity is most easy to describe in terms of how it feels and the sort of behaviours we should find within it.

A consultant who visited one organisation where an open culture had been created described its atmosphere in comparison with most other organisations as more alive, friendly, spontaneous and fun.

People laughed more and were in general:

- more prepared to raise questions
- more ready to address problem issues
- less restrained about thoughts or feelings.

Unpleasant issues still had to be dealt with. Disciplinary matters and performance problems were as likely to arise as in any organisation. People were still sometimes dismissed and jobs became redundant. However, the approach to dealing with such matters was in itself more honest and involving than is the norm in many organisations.

Within a culture for diversity, people should feel they can:

- speak honestly
- expect to be listened to
- take action to deal with problems at work.

The creation of such a culture is very challenging for managers at both individual and organisational levels. Listening to people involves dealing with the issues raised and takes time, effort and skill.

There is a natural human tendency towards achieving and maintaining equilibrium – a 'status quo'. Countering this tendency is difficult but worthwhile. For senior managers, in the words of a director involved in Shell's renewal initiative:

> '. . . the scariest part is letting go. You don't have the same kind of control that traditional leadership is used to. What you don't realise until you do it is that you

> may, in fact, have more controls, but in a different
> fashion. You get more feedback than before, you learn
> more than before, you know more through your own
> people about what's going on in the marketplace and
> with customers than before. But you still have to let go
> of the old sense of control.'
>
> Source: 'Surfing the edge of chaos', by Richard
> Pascale, *Sloan Management Review*, Spring 1999, p94.

Encouraging a process of constant challenge from within will
lead to greater inclusiveness, but will also involve radical
change and radical training to develop high degrees of
personal awareness at every level.

Summary

Today, we began by looking at our changing social context.
The importance of an open culture was explored and some of
the problems in achieving this were touched upon. Business
reasons for managing diversity in a constructive way were
illustrated, before we returned to stress the challenges of
achieving an open culture.

Tomorrow, we will put diversity in greater perspective as a
concept and distinguish between it and related approaches to
dealing with discrimination and difference. We will also
touch upon the links between good people management
practices, high performance and employee retention.

Diversity in perspective

Today, we will look at the development of ideas about diversity management and its background context. The need to learn from experience will be emphasised, together with the need for good people management practices to retain, as well as recruit, people from minorities.

Increased interest in diversity management

The management of diversity is a comparatively new area, with expertise being gradually built up through experience. There are many reasons for the interest in diversity, but most focus around the following issues:

- *Bottom line* – the so-called bottom line, or effect on financial performance, is especially important to business. Some organisations have found that successful diversity management leads to cost reductions, especially in terms of lower expenditure on recruitment and training.
- *Performance* – there is evidence of performance improvement and increased employee involvement within organisations where diversity increases. This is especially relevant for global project teams.
- *Legislation* – there are pressing legal reasons for fair recruitment and employment policies. Groups currently protected by legislation against employment discrimination include women, racial minorities and the disabled.
- *Morality* – discrimination against and exclusion of some groups of people from the workforce, or from more powerful job positions, has become a recognised social and moral problem within many organisations.

- *Public relations* – even if internal attitudes to and policies on fair recruitment and employment are backward, no organisation can now afford to be publicly recognised as discriminatory. In fact, most organisations see the benefits of becoming recognised as fair employers.
- *Learning and creativity* – it is increasingly understood that organisational learning and creativity require an open culture within which there is room for challenge and discussion, however uncomfortable.

The management of diversity can mean different things to different people. For some, it is understood in terms of multicultural integration and equal opportunities work. For others (as in this book), it is seen as:

- differing from an equal opportunities approach
- focusing on individual performance and the value of differences and differing contributions
- usually involving organisational culture change.

We need to distinguish clearly between affirmative action, equal opportunities programmes and diversity management before we go any further.

- *Affirmative action* – American affirmative action programmes give preference in recruitment or promotion to those from groups who are poorly represented at work or in senior management.
- *Equal opportunities* – these programmes focus on establishing equal opportunities for poorly represented groups and people in these groups may be treated differently to others, particularly in terms of special training being provided. When it comes to recruitment and selection, however, they will be treated on an equal footing with all others in the organisation.
- *Diversity management* – this approach aims to create an integrated, involved workforce from many different cultures, within which everyone is encouraged to develop and to perform to the limits of their own potential.

Affirmative action programmes and equal opportunities programmes, have gone some way towards overcoming workplace divisions. But, as discussed on Sunday, they have also created new problems and fail to deal directly with the reality of bias that guides human perception.

The diverse workplace

In a sense, western work organisations are becoming more diverse by default, as the make-up of our populations and the context of our business environments change. For example:

- Women now make up over half of the UK workforce if part-time workers are taken into account.
- Due to mergers and internationalisation, organisations are

becoming more global. We increasingly need to work abroad or with people from other countries and to link up with associates or customers abroad.

- In the United States, it is predicted that the number of white males entering the workforce will soon be a minority.

We need to develop diversity at work because our society is increasingly diverse. We also need to think about how we can manage diversity constructively and avoid the damage and other costs of discrimination. Failure to prevent harassing or discriminatory behaviour will:

- undermine the life quality of individual employees
- erode organisational performance
- possibly lead to high legal penalties
- inflate costs, through its inevitable damaging effects on:
  — labour turnover
  — organisational or team productivity
  — quality issues
  — communications
- lead to bad publicity.

Managing Workforce 2000
David Jamieson and Julie O'Mara
London, Jossey-Bass, 1991

Jamieson and O'Mara were among the first to offer strategies to manage an increasingly diverse workforce, identifying age, gender, ethnicity, education, disability and values as six perspectives on 'portraits of diversity'. They distinguish four main strategies to

implement their 'flex-management' approach:
1 matching people to jobs
2 performance management
3 employee communications and involvement
4 lifestyle and life needs support

Jamieson and O'Mara emphasise a policies- and systems-focused approach to change.

Diversity management – learning from experience

The management of diversity is a comparatively new area and people are still learning from experience and from mistakes. In the United States, where diversity management has been used more widely and for longer than anywhere else, diversity initiatives are often judged to be ineffective.

Diversity management in US organisations, 1991

As long ago as 1991, an ASTD national survey of Human Resource Development executives in Fortune 1000 companies found that 73 per cent were giving attention to diversity issues, suggesting that a connection was recognised between diversity and the bottom line at senior management levels. Of these:
• 11 per cent gave diversity high priority
• 29 per cent gave it moderate priority
• 33 per cent were just beginning to pay it attention.

Source: American Society for Training and Development.

In order to learn from experience, it is important to evaluate the success or failure of diversity management, but this is often a problem. During the 1980s and early 1990s, few organisations even tried to measure the effectiveness of their diversity programmes or training. Even now, measurement and evaluation remain difficult to achieve, but there are some relatively simple measures that can be used. Links between labour turnover and particular groupings, for example, can indicate costs or savings over time on recruitment and training.

Evidence linking high performance and good people management practice is now growing, and this suggests that effective diversity management will have performance benefits. Most of the specific practices mentioned by Pfeffer's research (see below), and the importance of community climate as described in research mentioned on Friday by the IPD (now the CIPD) will be relevant in creating a culture for diversity.

People really are our most important asset

In a 1999 article based on Pfeffer's book, *The Human Equation: Building Profits by Putting People First* (Boston, MA, Harvard Business School Press, 1998), Jeffrey Pfeffer and John Veiga draw together strong evidence of the business benefits of valuing people and improving management practices.

They refer to wide-scale research, linking:

- the use of high-performance practices **and** large gains in sales, market value and profits per employee
- improvements in human resource management systems **and** increased shareholder wealth per employee
- the value a company places on human resources **and** the probability of business survival over time.

Seven dimensions characterising systems producing profits through people are identified as:

1 employment security
2 selective hiring
3 self-managed teams and decentralisation
4 high compensation linked to business performance
5 extensive training
6 reduction of status differences
7 sharing information.

The authors acknowledge that, while these key dimensions may seem simple to apply, in practice there are many obstacles (especially short-termism) to their consistent implementation.

Source: 'Putting people first for organisational success, *Academy of Management Executive*, Vol 13 No 2, May 1999, pp37–48.

Winning and keeping new people

The message that inclusiveness can bring out the best potential of all employees, earn their working commitment and retain their services is far from new and links back to Elton Mayo's Hawthorne studies published in 1947 and the work of the human relations school of management. In addition:

- More contemporary work on staff retention suggests that people who do not feel included and accepted at work will become less involved and may seek alternative work.
- We know that the retention of women and people from minority groups can be a problem in many organisations.

Retention of black American employees

1 A 1999 US study of 1500 black women in 16 Fortune 1000 companies by Alignment Strategies found that 42 per cent of the respondents were seeking new jobs at the time of the study.
2 A Society of Black Engineers survey reported in 1999 found that 71 per cent of respondents were considering leaving their organisations due to poor quality supervision, stereotyping, lack of mentors, lack of job entitlement.

It is becoming clear that successfully managing diversity

involves not only encouraging job applications from minority groups but also working to keep successful applicants once they are in post.

Case study: achieving representative staffing at Asda

In opening a new store in Hulme, where there was a large ethnic population and extremely high unemployment, the need for staffing to reflect the local population was recognised and Asda sought to:

- target recruitment within the area
- ensure equal opportunities were open to all
- monitor turnover of staff and link this to managerial accountability
- empower staff more, particularly through the provision of a confidential helpline
- track the feelings of staff through attitude surveys.

The company used a local newspaper to advertise posts and formed links with community groups. Recruitment procedures were made less daunting and assistance was given on form-filling and interview skills.

Ethnic groups were not specifically targeted but most of the recruits (80 per cent in terms of visible identity) were from ethnic communities.

Source: 'Improving recruitment and promotion opportunities for ethnic minorities', *Equal Opportunities Review*, No 85, May/June 1999, pp15–20.

Summary

Today, we have summarised some of the reasons for increased interest in diversity management and distinguished between diversity, affirmative action and equal opportunities approaches to managing different groups. We looked at the need to reflect social diversity in the workplace and prevent discrimination, then acknowledged the problems of evaluating the effectiveness of diversity programmes. Lastly, the links between good practices in managing people and competitive performance were related to the association between increasing organisational diversity and improving competitive performance.

Before describing how change can be managed to help people become more aware of their attitudes and behaviour, it is important to understand the serious, structural implications of our failure to create a culture for diversity. Tomorrow, we will look at the effects of this failure on some more obvious minority groups.

For most of the week, however, our understanding of diversity management will be, first and foremost, as a focus on individuals and this will separate it from the group focus of an equal opportunities approach.

The divided workplace

For today, we will step back a little from diversity and look at the effects of discriminatory and stereotyping attitudes on particular groups. This will help us to understand the ingrained nature of discrimination and how it could also work against different groups to those discussed or even against the minority of one that we all potentially represent.

The groups we will concentrate on are those most blatantly affected by discrimination, even though protective legislation or a code of practice has been introduced to try to prevent this. They are:

- ethnic minority groups
- women
- disability groups
- age groups.

By focusing on these particular groups we can highlight the interaction between cultural exclusion and factors such as pay, promotion prospects, work status and unemployment.

Ethnic minorities at work

The differences in unemployment figures found by the 1997 Labour Force Survey for ethnic groups as compared with whites are too large to be coincidental:

- People from ethnic minorities were two and a half times more likely to be unemployed than the white population.
- The unemployment level for men of working age was 21

per cent for ethnic minorities compared with just over 8 per cent for whites.

- The 32 per cent unemployment rate for under-25s from ethnic minority groups was nearly three times that for comparable whites.

Yet such statistics conceal wide variations between and within ethnic groups, including different rates of unemployment and variations in education and qualifications between different ethnic groups. [Source: *Ethnic minorities in Britain: Diversity and disadvantage* by Tariq Modood et al., London, Policy Studies Institute, 1997.]

Most of us believe there is discrimination by employers against identifiable ethnic minorities and tests regularly show around a third of employers discriminate against job applicants from such groups.

Case study: harassment in the NHS

The early results of a research survey of NHS trusts by Plan for Action to Tackle Racial Harassment in the NHS were reported in April 2000. The survey found that around half of visible ethnic minority NHS staff claimed to have been racially harassed at work within the year previous to the survey. Around a half had witnessed racial harassment during the same period. Managers seemed unaware of the situation and expected few cases of harassment at work, yet most NHS ethnic minority employees see racial harassment from managers, colleagues, patients and the public as part of the job they do.

Few of the trusts surveyed had policies stating the objectives of reducing harassment at work, or providing training to deal with the problem.

While the picture is complex, there are some clear effects of ethnic group membership within the labour market. The mixed, overall message from research findings is that:

- ethnic group membership can be important and should be taken into account by employers . . .
- . . . but an individual cannot be considered first and foremost as a member of an ethnic minority group.

The glass ceiling for ethnic groups and women

In one important area it is still possible to generalise. Within large organisations and the professions, a 'glass ceiling' effect seems to operate against people from ethnic minorities, just as it has been found to operate against women. It is in the top 10 per cent of highest earning jobs that a broad division between ethnic minorities and whites as groups still seems valid. Men from all the ethnic minority groups were found to be seriously under-represented in this top 10 per cent.

Women, whether ethnic or white, are also under-represented at the top, although some companies are working hard to change this situation. Asda, for example, has worked to create a balanced representation of men and women in senior management and achieved a senior level made up of 40 per cent women and 60 per cent men.

This exclusion is also evidenced at the top in many professional groups.

The glass ceiling for women at the top

An April 2000 report in *Management Today* focused on Britain's 50 most powerful women. It claimed that, despite the Hansard Society's 1990 assertion that the 'glass ceiling' had to be broken and much effort on equal opportunities work by employers over 20 years, the glass ceiling remains only slightly cracked. The proportion of women in the boardroom has grown by only two per cent in the United Kingdom where, in 2000, Marjorie Scardino, CE of Pearsons, was still the only female chief executive of a FTSE-100 company. At the next level of quoted companies women bosses are still few and companies with one or two women on the board remain a rarity.

Even people from minority groups that show higher than average qualifications and earnings rarely gain a place in top boardrooms, so a big loss of talent at the top is suggested.

Women at work

Women are often targeted by equal opportunities policies. The profile of women in the workforce is changing fast, but there is still evidence of the different problems and obstacles faced by women in comparison with men.

Women no longer form so much of a minority in the workforce of western countries and are now better represented in most workplaces, in many professions and at most working levels.

A few have broken into board level executive work and increasing numbers are represented in management and at higher salary levels. Yet problems remain, particularly in the areas of pay, combining home and work responsibilities and cultural fit.

Pay
In 2000, a wide gap was still clear between men's and women's average earnings. Official sources gave the average earnings of men as 42 per cent higher than those of women and this seems to be the case across all occupations.

Evidence from particular professions often shows a marked difference between men's and women's pay and there seem to be some largely female and lower paid occupations.

Combining home and work responsibilities
Practical difficulties in balancing work and home life may

explain why many working women still tend to:

- work in particular professions, such as nursing or teaching
- take up particular types of work, such as cleaning or clerical work
- seek part-time rather than full-time hours
- work at home, for agencies or as casual employees.

It is most often women who need to resort to these forms of work because of their home role. Attracting and retaining women is closely linked to offering more flexible patterns of work and:

- taking account of employees' possible domestic or caring responsibilities
- discouraging a long hours culture
- offering part-time hours.

Case study: swapping roles

When a successful young Facilities Manager was expecting her first child, she and her husband decided that he would be the better carer, because he enjoyed children and the home, while his wife wanted to pursue her career and was the better paid of the two.
The arrangement was successful and the manager had three children in quick succession, keeping up her employment throughout. Both partners and their children were happy with the role swap and the only problem was a surprising one. The husband found that it was hard to establish friendships and associate casually with peers – the mothers of other children at school or

playgroup with his own – until they and their partners developed confidence in him. This only began to happen after the couple had lived in the area for long enough to become better known and more trusted.

Cultural fit

Harassment and discrimination against women is still often reported and can often be easily uncovered through surveys. The issue of women's equality in the workplace is very sensitive. Many people do not like to talk about it and some cannot discuss it without becoming emotional. Many women who achieve seniority say, if asked about it, that their gender has not been or is not an issue for them. Others have been known simply to state that they would prefer not to discuss it.

Unconsciously held attitudes – sometimes on the part of women as well as men – can underlie discriminatory behaviour. Within organisations, these attitudes can be so built into the existing culture, structure and processes that they are difficult to recognise from the inside. Discrimination in this context becomes very subtle and hard to pin down. Sometimes, it may have concrete effects in the form of staff turnover amongst women. More often, it may have hidden effects that can only be detected by listening to women, such as:

- experiences of isolation
- the requirement to adapt or restrain behaviour to achieve acceptance.

Women sometimes find, for example, that levels of assertiveness accepted from men are not acceptable from women.

Case study: appearances count?

A woman interviewed for a shelf-filler's post in a rural branch of a well-known retail store had a nose-stud, brightly coloured streaks in her hair and a masculine style of dress. She told her interviewer that she only wanted the job if she could wear trousers and heavy boots for work, as she was most comfortable in this form of dress. The store was short of staff and the woman seemed enthusiastic, so the interviewing personnel officer agreed that she could wear boots and trousers, as long as she also wore the store overall.

The woman worked well, but a visiting Regional Manager objected about her appearance and suggested she should be asked to wear a skirt and normal shoes for work. The personnel officer had to pass this on as an order, but later obtained agreement that the shelf-filler could wear a pair of the store's male uniform trousers and her boots. By then, the woman had found another job.

Nationally, the store in question had long-established equal opportunities policies and was seeking to implement a diversity management strategy.

Disability groups

From 1990 in the United States and 1995 in the United Kingdom, legislative requirements have reinforced the social need to employ more people with disabilities, or enable continued employment, where possible, if existing employees become disabled.

Disabled people of working age in the UK in 2000 comprised 18.7 per cent of the working population but only 12 per cent of the employed population.

Employers' own estimates of the number of disabled people in the workplace are typically around two per cent, according to an Industrial Relations Services survey of organisations in July 2000. [Source: 'Managing disability at work', by John Ballard, *IRS Employment Review*, No 18].

UK Government support for employers

Information, support and advice for UK employers on disability issues is available through the Employment Service's disability service teams. The Government's Access to Work scheme offers financial help for employers who need to deal with the additional needs of some disabled employees.
The service teams and the Access to Work scheme can be contacted through local Job Centre offices.

UK Government guidance on good practice for managing disability recommends monitoring to help plan for the future, focusing on:

- number of job applications received from disabled people
- number and level of promotions for disabled people
- expenditure on, and usefulness of, adjustments made in the workplace to accommodate disabled people
- training on disability awareness provided for employees.

Some employers go beyond the requirements of the law in employing disabled people and their positive policies are likely to include:

- guaranteeing interviews for disabled applicants
- welcoming applications from disabled people in recruitment advertisements
- offering information about vacant posts in alternative formats, such as audio tapes.

The IRS survey mentioned above found that most large employers now have policies to promote equal opportunities for the disabled and make use of available help and advice services. But the number monitoring disabilities or comprehensively assessing premises and policies for disability remains low.

Checklist
Making life easier for wheelchair users

Some provisions to help wheelchair users at work are reasonably obvious, but there are many smaller things that can improve the environment for them, as the

---

following checklist shows.

1 Bars and counter heights need to be low enough for wheelchair users.

2 Files and equipment should be just above or below the wheelchair user's shoulder height, to be easily reachable.

3 Desks and tables should be checked for potential obstacles, such as bars across the legs.

4 The static position of wheelchair users means they get cold quickly and easily, so their warmth needs to be considered.

5 Offices, corridors and access points should be kept clear of permanent or temporary obstacles.

6 Look at internal as well as external doors and how they might cause problems – where possible, ensure they are not double, heavy or without handles.

7 Try to replace carpets with other covering in areas that are heavily used by people in wheelchairs, as they will find carpets harder to traverse.

8 Remember that the recommended weight for manual handling is far lower than for standing personnel – at 5 kg.

9 The effects of being permanently at a much lower eye level than standing people can be uncomfortable – when possible, sit down to talk to a wheelchair user on his or her own level.

The need to employ more disabled people and to think about making work more accessible for employees, clients or customers who are disabled is an increasingly important aspect of diversity management and planning.

Age groups at work

Ageism is connected to disablement, in that older workers can be more susceptible to disabilities and many cases based on disability discrimination have involved dismissals of older people after long-term absence. Recognition of age discrimination is relatively new and it did not become a big issue in the UK until quite recently, as:

- a trend towards 'early exit' from employment for older workers (often due to redundancy) became recognised
- the need to adapt to an overall ageing population began to affect policy considerations.

The main focus during the 1990s was on how ageism seems to consistently disadvantage older people more in terms of unemployment and vocational or developmental training. Ageism does not just mean discrimination against older workers, however. In 2000, the UK Employers Forum on Age (EFA) found that almost half of younger workers surveyed (aged 18 to 30) felt age discrimination against youth had been an obstacle blocking their career progression.

A diversity approach involves guarding against all age-based barriers or discrimination and:

- seeking a mixed age balance for the workforce as a whole
- being aware of potential, general differences between differing age groups or generations
- looking at people first and foremost as individuals and avoiding the use of age as a basis for promotion, recruitment or training provision.

Summary

Today, we have looked at workplace discrimination against ethnic minorities, women, disability groups and older or younger people. We have also indicated the extent to which discrimination can affect individual lives and prospects for people who belong to one of these or a similar minority group, due to lower employment, pay and promotion rates.

Tomorrow, we will start to consider how we might work to change attitudes and organisational cultures, with the aim of preventing the disadvantages for individuals and the performance limitations for organisations that are caused by discrimination and stereotyping.

Towards a culture for everyone

Today, we will begin to consider how it is possible to change a culture so that diversity can develop. We will look at:

> * ideas about culture
> * psychological approaches to understanding culture
> * how these feed into creating training and policies to support change.

We will lay the plan for our phased approach to cultural change and work through the first phase – gaining leadership and involvement from senior executives.

What is culture?

Culture is an intangible element that is difficult to define and some people still do not accept that it exists, let alone how important it can be. Yet culture is generally considered a key factor in understanding how organisations work and change. Sometimes described as the 'glue' that holds an organisation together, or the insider's appreciation of 'the way we do things round here', culture is:

* shaped by our past and learning
* formed from a pattern of commonly held attitudes, values, beliefs and assumptions.

Edgar Schein, one of the first management theorists to define corporate culture, saw it as a mix of factors. His influential 1985 model of culture explains that it is manifest at surface, middle and deepest levels.

Surface level

Here, culture is both **enacted** and **reinforced** through visible appearances and behaviours, such as physical layouts, dress codes, organisational structure, company policies, procedures and programmes and attitudes and behaviours.

Attitudes are the established ways of responding to people and situations that we have learned, based on the values, beliefs and assumptions that we hold. Attitudes become manifest through our behaviour – what we say and do. In an organisation, attitudes can be better understood through identifiable symbols, metaphors, stories, rituals and ceremonies.

Middle level

At this level, culture is manifested through our:

- *values* – how we have learnt to think things ought to be or people ought to behave, especially in terms of qualities such as honesty, integrity and openness
- *beliefs* – how we think things really are, what we think is really true and what we therefore expect as likely consequences that will follow from our behaviour.

Deepest level

Here, culture is manifested through **basic assumptions** – our long-learnt, automatic responses and established opinions. We are, ourselves, almost always unaware of the nature of our own basic assumptions, but they are enacted through our behaviour.

Basic assumptions are usually rooted in our infancy, early family life and social context. More widely, assumptions shaping our behaviour can relate to national context. In western society as a whole, for example, we take it for granted that human beings have an individualist nature, but in other societies, things may be different. In Japanese society, for instance, individualism is less pronounced. Perceptions and behaviours differ from those of westerners as a result of the assumption that people are fundamentally connected and duty towards all others is a very serious matter.

Culture and group behaviour – a brief glossary

Rituals – Routine, informal activities and procedures that, through repetition, develop a special but unconscious significance within an organisation, which insiders will intuitively recognise and which will 'encode' information and relationships. Rituals might include, for example, the greeting of new recruits by the Managing Director.

Symbols – These can be important indicators of:
- success or status, such as company cars, allotted parking spaces, eating arrangements or approved qualifications and titles
- corporate image, for example workplace design and furnishings – a high reception counter, for instance, is forbidding and suggests limited access to outsiders.

Stories – The stories people tell within an organisation carry messages for newcomers, customers and outsiders. These can assume mythic proportions and build up people or events from the past to a heroic status.

Ceremonies – Formal celebratory or award-based events and activities will differ in type and frequency etc between organisations.

Group think – This can occur when people in an established group let group consensus and loyalty over-ride realistic appraisal and individual opinions or feelings.

Stereotyping – We place people into categories on the basis of information about them and from clues such as accent or appearance. This can help us to learn from experience and deal better with others in some respects, but it is also limiting, in that we seem to assume far too much about individuals on the basis of limited visual or verbal information, such as their age or where they studied. Most of us are also selective in our perceptions, seeing only things that support our initial perception and failing to perceive contradictory data.

Roles – Roles are strongly linked to stereotyping, as we tend to assume stereotypical characteristics that attach to people in given roles, whether these are work, social or family roles. If we contradict the expectations others have of our role we are likely to cause some confusion and resentment.

An organisational culture is complex and can encompass many sub-cultures but tends to be shared to at least some degree by people within it. If there is a great difference between a newcomer's existing assumptions and those operating within the organisation, the new person may leave quickly or become part of a sub-cultural group. Those who remain within an organisation usually come, over time, to share in and reinforce its existing culture.

How do we learn culture?

The way in which human beings learn culture is complex, but some brief background on the psychology should help us to understand the difficulties involved in changing organisations.

We tend to assume that we are able to control our perceptions, thoughts and behaviours but several strands of psychology combine to suggest this is not always so. These include:

- Behaviourism
- Maslow's motivational theory
- Constructionism
- Psychodynamics and emotion
- Social constructionism.

These ideas and approaches are not easy to assimilate, but all help to explain the forces that drive us.

Behaviourism
Behaviourism is based on the linking of events or experiences so that one elicits the response of the other, leaving no room for our thought or control. Such a 'conditioned' response can occur naturally, and can also be manipulated through the use of stimuli events to direct conditioned responses.

Behaviourism suggests that much learning is an unconscious process of conditioning linked to rewards or reinforcement.

Maslow's motivational theory
Abraham Maslow's motivational theory is still influential and links to both behaviourism and psychodynamics. In 1943, Maslow suggested a hierarchy of needs that we are all driven to try to fulfil to achieve satisfaction. These operate in

a serial way, so that basic needs such as hunger have to be fulfilled first. The need to belong and receive recognition is a powerful driving force within us all, especially when we join a new group, department or organisation.

As we seek to fit in and belong, we become more susceptible to 'operant conditioning'. This makes us more likely to pick up and learn the attitudes, values, beliefs and assumptions of others around us. In an organisational setting, this means we will unconsciously be learning and adapting to try to fit in with the existing corporate culture.

Constructionism
The behaviourist and motivational approaches provide some explanation of how we learn attitudes and behaviour, especially in terms of our skills and habitual ways of thinking and responding. Constructionism can add to this, and is based on the idea that we construct sequences of thought and action from experience. From birth, these mental constructs act as building blocks for our learning and development.

Our basic constructs change as we learn, then at a certain point the structure of the construct 'reforms' into a new entity. These processes, particularly 'reforming', are what we usually recognise as change.

Where there is only outside pressure for change or conformity, resulting changes are likely to be superficial and our old views quickly reassert themselves when the influence or pressure to change is removed. Many change programmes fail because existing constructs are not really reformed. People's understanding and belief have not been properly engaged and they have 'played' (consciously or unconsciously) at going along with the attempted changes.

Psychodynamics and emotions
Emotions are critical and can be a major obstacle to change.
The unique concepts of psychodynamics attempt to explain
the drives behind behaviour in terms of:

• early infant and childhood experience
• the profound influence of 'significant others'
• the continuing power of these within our subconscious
• the controlling force of the subconscious in our behaviours.

From the perspective of psychodynamics, much of what we
do is designed to reduce our own internal anxiety and
maintain at least our illusions of control. We learn 'templates'
for relating to people and situations, often very early in
childhood. This learning acts like programming deep within
our subconscious, affecting us in the same way as a
computer's operating system, running the show behind the
scenes and shaping our responses and behaviours.

Social constructionism

Behaviourism and constructionism focus on the individual, viewing:

- learning as an internal, mental process locked into an individual mind
- the person as a separate unit, apart from others
- the mind as self-contained
- the personality as a singular entity, with one set of more or less consistent traits.

To return to a computing analogy, people are seen as stand-alone personal computers, cut off from others in their functioning.

This view is now seriously challenged, however, by a further approach known as social constructionism, which sees people more as open, networked systems, linked to each other and their surrounding culture. From this perspective, we are constantly changing and reconstructing through our social interaction with others, and from an early age take as our own the ideas and attitudes of 'significant others' around us.

This means that influences we have picked up from others, but which we are not usually conscious of, can create one of the main barriers to a culture for diversity. A child, for example, picks up deep and lasting attitudes and prejudices through the words and actions of parents and others, long before he or she is capable of evaluation.

Social constructionism emphasises learning as a social process. What we know and who we become is strongly influenced by others with whom we mix. We learn from others' intentions, feelings, values and beliefs. We also learn through interactions within the organisation and the meanings embedded in them.

Social constructionism suggests that, in a sense, the people and culture around us become a part of us, affecting what we think and how we behave.

The implications for cultural change

Even this whistle-stop tour of psychological theories can hopefully illustrate that:

- we are bound to have acquired much bias and prejudice from our surroundings
- we will usually find it difficult to 'see through' the acquired and deeply established baggage that shapes our views of the world and our responses to others
- no real and permanent behavioural change can be achieved without beginning to understand, and deal with, our heritage of sometimes limiting bias and prejudice and its often negative effects.

Social constructionism, however, offers a new dimension of hope for successful individual change. If we have become who we are through acquiring attitudes, beliefs, values and assumptions during social interaction, and this process is continuous, then change can be viewed as a more open, interconnected process.

This prospect is immensely significant in terms of organisational change and the possibility of developing a culture for diversity. It suggests that, by carefully reconstructing the socialisation process, we can probably acquire differing attitudes, beliefs, values and assumptions.

This idea is key in the process of creating a culture for diversity which we will now go on to develop.

Approaching change: setting course

The four-phase approach we will take to developing a culture for diversity will be:

1   Initiating change – the Senior Management Team seminar
2   Evaluation – 'where we are now'
3   The hardware of change – systems, structures and processes
4   The software of change – changing people and culture

We will consider phase one today and continue through the phases for the rest of the week.

Phase one – SMT seminar on the potential benefits of a programme for diversity

The need for greater diversity is usually recognised by one person, such as a human resources or personnel manager. To move into action, however, the agreement, involvement and commitment of the senior management team (SMT) has to be gained. If the Chief Executive accepts that greater diversity would benefit the organisation, successful action will be easier to achieve. But winning commitment from all managers may still be a difficult task and is vital to effect long-term change.

Achieving diversity – force or persuasion?

The slow progress of diversity issues has led some people to suggest more forceful approaches. In 2000:

- The Chairman of the Post Office talked of favouring the use of 'reverse discrimination' to get more women into senior positions.
- The Government insisted that police forces meet ethnic minority targets in officer recruitment.

Impatience is understandable yet in terms of developing a culture for diversity that carries people with it, any enforcement of set standards or quotas (especially if imposed from outside an organisation) would mean that:

- 'free choice' would be minimal
- commitment would therefore be limited or non-existent.

Under such circumstances, people may just go along with programmes and changes because they have no alternative, rather than because they believe in what is being attempted. At the worst, some may try to deliberately undermine the programme of change.

To gain leadership commitment, phase one of the programme involves the change agent meeting the SMT in a seminar aimed at convincing them of the benefits of change. The presentation should progress in a structured way through:

1 *Knowledge* – what is a diverse culture?
2 *Comprehension* – understanding in greater depth the

meaning of diversity.

3 *Application* – applying the concept of diversity to your organisation and evaluating what it could mean for us.

4 *Assessment of need* – analysing the negative consequences of not having a diverse culture or the real risk of costly claims and bad PR from discrimination cases.

The initial part of the seminar should be informative in style, giving background to:

- raise the level of SMT awareness about what is meant by 'a culture for diversity'
- develop SMT understanding of why the business should devote time and resources to establishing such a culture
- establish a common language and mutual understanding.

Emphasis should be placed upon **key issues** in developing a more diverse organisation, the possible **negative consequences** of doing nothing and the potential **positive consequences** of taking steps towards achieving greater diversity.

Once a common level of knowledge is reached, details of the proposed change programme can be discussed more informally, to involve people and encourage them to 'buy into' the programme of their own volition.

A focusing question is:

What type of diverse culture does the organisation require to achieve its purpose?

This makes it clear that diversity is a strategic business issue and is not just concerned with ensuring the rights of one or another group of people. It should help people to develop discussion of the strategic importance of a diverse culture and reduce the more emotive responses sometimes associated with equal opportunities.

A lesson many people refuse to learn is that individuals are more likely to own and protect what they are involved in creating. For this reason, the participation of key managers is critical to achieve a minimum level of commitment and further action.

This phase is only a beginning. Even if the SMT are genuinely committed to developing a diverse culture, there is a big difference between them thinking it a good idea and actually doing things differently enough to effect change. Research and experience both show that managers can wreck their own change programmes, especially when there is a clear inconsistency between what they say and what they do.

Classification and control

In many ways, organisations are similar to small societies. M Douglas' framework for understanding aspects of culture in society has been adapted to highlight aspects of culture within an organisation. The model has two dimensions: **Classification** and **Control.**

'Classification' applies to the main system of ideas and meanings in the organisation. For example, a common judgement, such as 'all IT people are poor communicators', might be part of such a system. 'Control' is the pressure to conform with dominant values, ideas and attitudes. Within an organisation, this pressure is likely to come largely from senior management, in the form of both direct orders, indirect procedures and (often unspoken) rules.

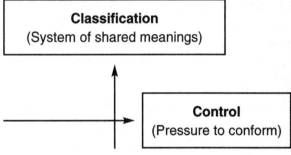

Figure one: Classification and Control

High control indicates strong pressure to conform to the expectations of the dominant parties. This could be reflected, for example, in a senior manager actually finding complaints made about discrimination or harassment objectionable, even though the organisation's policies promote equal opportunities and protection from harassment.

If an organisation has high levels of classification and control the emphasis will be firmly on conformity, probably discipline and intolerance of difference. To change such an organisation, not only the system of ideas and meanings but also senior attitudes and values will need to change to balance the new system. Both the classification and the control aspects will need to be changed simultaneously.

Source: *Explorations in Cosmology* by M Douglas, 3rd edn, London, Routledge & Kegan Paul, 1996.

Summary

Our objective today has been to deepen our understanding of organisational culture and how we learn within it, often in an involuntary way. Our discussion of the social constructionist perspective on development as a more open process led into the increased possibilities this implies for change. We concluded by outlining phase one of the course we are setting towards change – the SMT seminar.

Tomorrow, we will go through phase two, evaluation of the current situation, and then move on to the 'hardware' side of change, starting on phase three – adapting structures, systems and processes to support cultural change.

The hardware of change

Today, we will concentrate on implementing phases two and three of our approach to developing a culture for diversity:

- evaluating 'where we are now'
- beginning to implement the 'hardware of change' – changing systems, structures and processes to support cultural change.

After discussing how we can approach evaluation (our phase two), a model will be presented to illustrate our understanding of the interactive relationship between organisational culture and the three linked areas of purpose, infrastructure and people.

We will then start to look at processes and structures (phase three) and the contribution they can make to the management of diversity.

Phase two – Evaluation: identifying the current position

Having achieved at least a minimal level of senior commitment, the next phase is to assess the current position and look beyond symptoms to underlying problems. For example, it is pointless changing one aspect of the organisation, such as recruiting policy, only to lose any new staff recruited because they find the culture hostile.

Someone external to the organisation will be better placed to carry out the evaluation, as an internal person will be susceptible to organisational blindspots and vulnerable within the context of the emotive issues involved. But internal evaluators, reporting directly to the Chief Executive, will have an important role acting as the CE's eyes and ears in keeping him or her alert to what is felt and what is happening throughout the organisation.

Begin by examining factors that can help and hinder the development of a more diverse culture. For example, look at:

- existing policies and procedures and whether they need to change to give more support to diversity objectives
- the composition of the existing workforce and its current make-up in terms of different groups, focusing on areas such as gender, age, disability, class, race or education
- predominant leisure interests and sporting activities, where possible, especially of senior managers, so that linked social networks based on activities, such as golf, tennis or rugby, can be checked for their possible effects on recruitment or promotion.

Case study: Coca-Cola – the dangers of informal networks

Coca-Cola gives strong backing to civil rights, but at its headquarters blacks were poorly represented. The first black senior manager was appointed in the 1980s and the only non-white executive was reported as almost having retired in January 2000 because of being passed over for promotions.
He changed his mind but problems remained within the company, including impending cases for abuse or discrimination. Ex-employees have stressed Coca-Cola's insularity at senior levels, with people (usually men) from the University of Georgia having filled many positions in the past.
A new CEO has pledged to link one quarter of managers' pay to their performance on stated goals to develop greater diversity. But achieving more balanced racial representation and more aware attitudes within the company will take time.

Source: 'Coke: say good-bye to the good ol' boy culture' by Dean Foust, *Business Week*, 29 May 2000, p49.

At a deeper level, seek out aspects of the culture that will affect diversity and identify relevant values, attitudes and beliefs and how they come through in behaviour. To understand the underlying rites, rituals, symbols and ceremonies that shape behaviour, look for patterns and attitudes represented in existing routines. For example:

- how work is organised
- the conduct of meetings
- the nature of regular, established group gatherings
- whether and how any order of deference operates.

Questionnaires to explore attitudes and cultural climates tend to be superficial and give no measure of rituals, symbols or deference routines. Other methods can provide more qualitative data about what is happening and how people feel:

- *critical incident analysis* – the identification and analysis of critical incidents connected to problems related to diversity issues, such as harassment or discrimination
- *interviews* – semi-structured interviews with key and/or randomly selected people
- *participant observation/ethnography* – sharing insiders' interactions and activities
- *focus groups* – discussions centred on exploring ideas and feelings on given issues.

Human resources systems

Systems need to be adapted or redesigned to monitor areas where unintentional discrimination affecting particular groups can be most easily detected. These areas include:

- the ratios of staff from different groups who are selected for:
  — promotion
  — training
  — allocation to projects and special teams
- labour turnover
- performance appraisals
- grievances.

Once the implementation of diversity measures is accepted, a tracking system to monitor numbers recruited from different groups and retention figures for them is a necessity, if the effectiveness of the strategy is to be evaluated.

Case study: Lloyds TSB recruitment tracking

Lloyds TSB introduced a tracking system in 1997 to ensure policies to recruit more ethnic graduates were working. In 1999, the company also monitored retention issues by distinguishing ethnic and minority groupings in a survey of the barriers facing all employees. From the survey it was found that, while the same barriers affected everyone, they had more impact for groups such as ethnic minorities and women.

As a result, the company is now looking at whether managers could help to retain more people by learning to manage the differences between varied groups, such as part-time workers, older workers, the disabled, ethnic minorities and others.

Source: 'Improved recruitment and promotion opportunities for ethnic minorities', *Equal Opportunities Review*, No 85, May/June 1999, pp15–20.

Holistic change – strategy, infrastructure and people

The evaluation and the resulting implementation of changes should be holistic in nature, covering all aspects of an organisation. Figure two, shown below, identifies key areas that need to be addressed if meaningful change is to occur.

Like a three-legged stool, each supporting and inter-relating area should also support the central area of organisational culture.

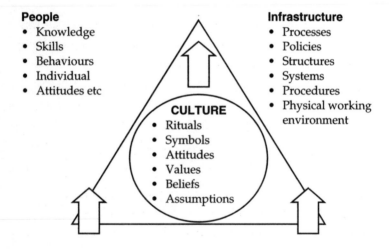

Purpose
- Vision
- Strategy
- Espoused values

People
- Knowledge
- Skills
- Behaviours
- Individual
- Attitudes etc

Infrastructure
- Processes
- Policies
- Structures
- Systems
- Procedures
- Physical working environment

CULTURE
- Rituals
- Symbols
- Attitudes
- Values
- Beliefs
- Assumptions

Figure two: A model for changing organisational culture

Purpose
Strategic issues, such as vision, goals and policies, should all support a diverse culture and 'big picture' issues have to be addressed, as below. Key questions to ask when considering your strategy for diversity are:

- Is managing diversity included in the corporate strategy?
- Has a clear statement been made from the top about commitment to diversity and what is expected from people?
- Who is responsible for diversity?
- Do existing policies support diversity?
- How is diversity evaluated?
- Is there a willingness to commit resources to long-term development?

Take care not to allow discussion to create an illusion of having brought about change. Sometimes, strategy formulation does not go beyond the level of ritual.

To prevent this from happening, periodic evaluation should push strategy through. After ensuring that a strategy is being implemented, key factors to consider are:

- Who has helped or hindered in implementing the strategy?
- How effective has the strategy been?
- Have the costs of implementation been within budget?
- What have we learnt from it?

These issues may raise awkward questions relating to personal performance and will provoke anxiety, but they cannot be avoided if the strategy is to be realised.

Infrastructure
This is the area we will go on to look at more closely today – the 'hardware' of change. New or adapted systems, structures and processes will not bring about change in themselves but they will support cultural change and they need to be consistent with strategic direction in underpinning diversity objectives.

People

People's behaviour, attitudes, feelings and involvement are all key to and interact with an organisation's culture. They are central to the 'software' part of our course for change and we will concentrate on this area on Friday and Saturday.

Having illustrated the interplay between culture and the three main cultural supports of strategy, infrastructure and people, we will move on to the role of systems, structures and processes, or infrastructure, in supporting cultural change.

Phase three – implementing the hardware of change: key processes and diversity

Some key processes to look at during the remainder of today will be managing grievances, recruitment and selection, reward and performance management, training and development, internal communications and flexible working.

Managing grievances – learning through problems

Perhaps the most important support in establishing a more open, diverse culture is an effective grievance procedure, so we will discuss this at some length. The term now has very negative associations, so we will distinguish here between traditional grievance procedures and our own version, which we will call **resolution procedures**.

A 'resolution procedure' involves more than the traditional approach to grievances. It describes an internal mechanism to encourage staff to raise issues about which they feel aggrieved or concerned, and to make complaints. In essence, employees' complaints should be treated in the same way that enlightened service operators treat customer complaints

– as issues to explore, resolve and learn from. Resolution procedures provide individuals with an informal, anonymous way to bring about change.

All complaints should be recorded on an anonymous basis, unless or until it becomes necessary to move into a formal grievance stage, involving names and details. The resulting record of anonymous complaints will be invaluable in terms of letting us know what is really happening and how people feel within the organisation. Resolution procedures should only move into named and formally recorded stages when the parties involved and others within the organisation are unable to resolve the matter, and further judgement is required within (or through legal processes outside) the organisation.

In terms of creating a culture for diversity, listening to and attempting to resolve complaints at an early stage will:

• establish trust and improve employee relations
• reveal any discriminatory behaviours, policies or practices affecting employees
• lead to possible preventative rather than punitive action to deal with problem areas.

Resolution procedures should encourage people to raise and discuss issues of concern, drawing complaints and whistle-blowing matters into the arena for discussion before they become entrenched problems.

Establishing a procedure that allows staff to raise an issue and see it handled effectively is critical if a culture of diversity is to be achieved and the organisation is to learn from mistakes. The use of resolution procedures can, in a controlled way, create the sort of creative instability in an organisation or department that we discussed on Monday. Pascale has argued that if things go too well and there is no contention within an organisation it is in danger of losing its edge. A resolution procedure will cause questions to be asked and involve repeated examination of the values, beliefs and core assumptions that comprise an organisation's culture. It can, therefore, provide an effective feedback loop for organisational reflection and learning.

Constructive conflict within Honda

Honda has institutionalised sessions known as Weigaya sessions, with the Japanese word Weigaya signifying the sound of heated discussion. These are suggested when people seem to be holding back and meetings have lost their impulsion and energy. During a Weigaya session, rank ceases to matter. Participants are expected to raise 'undiscussable' issues that are likely to involve disagreement and argument (without personalising these issues).

Source: 'The benefit of a clash of opinions', by Richard T Pascale, *Personnel Management*, Vol 25 No 10, October 1993, pp38–41.

Recruitment and selection

Recruitment is too important to be left to the chance choices or instincts of untrained people. A well-communicated code of practice should give clear guidelines to prevent discrimination and set objective standards for selection. Training for recruitment can draw diversity issues into such areas as:

- relevant legislation
- shortlisting
- the business benefits of unbiased recruitment advertising
- the use of person specifications
- decision-making
- the design of an appropriate selection procedure
- interviewing
- bases for questioning
- effective listening
- questioning techniques.

Recruitment quotas for particular groups may be necessary to build up a diverse workforce. But, as discussed on Monday, keeping people who are recruited is equally important and holding onto those with the greatest potential for high performance is even more of a challenge.

Case study: graduate recruitment at Lloyds TSB

Lloyds TSB used focus groups to investigate a lack of ethnic graduate job applicants. It was found that banking was unattractive to them because advertising literature showed a mostly white workforce. Also, it was viewed as a stuffy environment, part of a white, male establishment.

The merger between Lloyds Bank and TSB underlined the need for a more diverse recruitment strategy because TSB had a wider customer base than Lloyds. The need to reflect this in terms of staffing was considered urgent.

Lloyds TSB changed its advertising literature to include people from diverse backgrounds, showing them at home as well as at work. Case studies about ethnic graduates were included with contact details.

Advertisements were placed in the ethnic press and relevant language skills were sought in recruitment. The company's 1998-99 training investment included cross-cultural awareness for branch managers.

The percentage of ethnic minority graduates recruited had increased from four to 16 per cent by 1997 and to 19 per cent by 1998.

Source: 'Improved recruitment and promotion opportunities for ethnic minorities', *Equal Opportunities Review*, No 85, May/June 1999, pp15–20.

Reward and performance management
Linking performance to aspects of diversity, such as respecting

individuals and treating them fairly, will build diversity issues more integrally into an organisation's strategy and mission. If people are accountable on specific issues and their performance is linked to rewards, these issues will assume more importance. To link diversity into performance management:

- set annual goals related to diversity
- appraise the situation regularly
- adapt policies and goals in line with the findings.

Training and development
A visible commitment to diversity can be shown through long-term training and development policy within organisations.

Managers' training is especially important as their behaviour can have far-reaching effects on others.

Awareness training, like the Multi-Dimensional Training discussed on Saturday, can develop consciousness of prejudicial attitudes and behaviour and of the impact of this on others within the organisation.

Once people have bought into diversity for themselves the focus can move on to other issues, such as different religions, functional skills cultures and facts and issues relating to diversity.

Internal communications
Many communications activities can support a culture of diversity, simply by raising the profile of issues and keeping them at the front of people's minds. Conventional communications, such as internal house journals, briefings and mission statements, can be used. New communications elements specifically aimed at supporting diversity could also be initiated. For example:

- profiles of individuals from different groups
- reminders of the offensiveness and illegality of discrimination
- news articles from people with relevant experience.

The resolution procedures discussed earlier would act as a central communications channel, giving information on feelings within the organisation and enabling positive feedback.

Flexible working
Flexible working patterns will help most employees achieve a good work/life balance, and help those who need to care for young or ill family members to continue to work and perform well. Flexible working practices include:

- career breaks
- job-sharing
- part-time work
- term-time working
- partial retirement
- special leave for special occasions
- home-working possibilities
- more flexible hours or flexitime
- annualised, rather than weekly, hours.

Sometimes, however, flexibility can be limited in practice and promises of highly flexible hours may be revealed as limited after the job has been accepted. To avoid the staff loss this can cause, be realistic in describing the flexible options open to recruits.

Summary

Today, we have covered phase two, evaluating the current situation with regard to diversity, and outlined the model from which our course for change is derived. We began to work through phase three, adapting the 'hardware' of systems, structures and processes to support a culture for diversity. We then introduced an approach to managing grievances that can contribute greatly to the development of diversity, as well as resolving complaints.

Tomorrow, we will complete our phase three focus on the hardware of change by looking at some processes or structures that could be introduced to support diversity. We will then begin to look at the concepts underlying the MDT training approach, to be outlined on Saturday.

From hardware to software – people and change

Today, we will look at some of the new systems, structures and processes that you may wish to introduce to help build a more diverse organisation, such as:

- continuing policy review
- measuring the benefits of diversity
- self-help networks
- mentoring
- discussion or focus groups.

We will then begin on the all-important phase four of our course for change. We will expand upon how our view of organisations can lead us to downplay human issues and culture, when these are of central importance, especially in making changes. We will then outline how four essential elements set the foundations for a Multi-Dimensional Training programme:

1 a safe learning environment
2 a group context
3 feedback
4 facilitation skills.

New processes or structures to support diversity

Continuing policy review
Continuing policy review involves checking existing formal

and informal policies and is critical to combat institutionalised discrimination. This can build up in the thousands of policies that accumulate over time, especially in a large organisation. A process of systematic evaluation of policies by human resource specialists would be the most thorough approach to check for potentially discriminatory effects.

Case study: institutionalised discrimination in action

In the police service, bullet-proof vests made for men were purchased for use by all officers. During a review stemming from a grievance it become obvious that this was discriminatory, in that women found the protective vests uncomfortable. This routine purchase of male equipment was one example among many of an unwitting form of discrimination against people with small hands, which affected women in particular.

Measuring the benefits of diversity

This is a difficult area, as many potential benefits of diversity management relate to culture, morale and life quality, rather than hard-nosed results. Cost benefits from savings on recruitment and selection can be accounted for over time, while there are companies that have linked sales benefits to their diversity strategies. Look out for areas where benefits can be shown and measured, seeking hard data that shows links to revenues where possible.

Self-help networks

Self-help networks for groups who are in a minority, or feel themselves to be discriminated against, can enable people to create a source of support for themselves. This kind of activity is important as isolation can lead people from minority groups to feel unaccepted, and to seek another job.

While some assistance may be needed to set up and organise networks initially, they can quickly become quite self-sufficient if they are successful, and provide an invaluable source of 'inside' information on issues affecting minorities.

Mentoring

Mentoring can be an important support approach, and involves established people within the organisation acting as 'mentors' or coaches for one or two years to new recruits or to employees who want developmental support. Mentors keep in regular contact with their 'mentees', follow their progress and give practical and moral support.

A mentoring scheme can either be informal or linked to a formal development programme. For those from minority groups, it can be helpful if their mentor understands the particular problems associated with their background.

Discussion or focus groups

Informal or formal employee discussion groups can be an excellent communications approach for improving general management. Where increased diversity is sought, they can be used to explore issues that can move diversity forward.

In the United States, many organisations set up equality councils to enable employees to become involved in developing a fairer working environment for all and to raise awareness of diversity issues.

*Case study: American President Lines Limited –
dialoguing to reinforce diversity*

At American President Lines Limited, a diversity
programme was largely based on recruitment, training
and development work. It was felt something more was
necessary to give the issues more meaning.

Dialoguing is based on a year-long commitment by
interested employees to monthly, two-hour discussion
groups that are extremely frank, facilitated by trained
staff and focus on any difference issues.

The lengthy meetings and year-long commitment are
important, as people can become defensive during
discussions and their feelings need to be worked
through. Groups work best, according to the
organisation's Director of Diversity, when they include a
good cross-sample of people of differing race, gender,
age, sexual orientation, personality and geographical
and educational background.

Unusual bonds form and members begin to focus on
who people are as individuals rather than how they can
be easily classified. As a result, links are made for work
purposes – problem-solving, project teams or
promotions, for example – that would never have
occurred without dialoguing.

Source: 'The harsh reality of diversity' by Gillian Flynn,
Workforce, Vol 77 No 12, December 1998, pp42–44,
46, 49.

Linking into the software

The organisational 'hardware' issues discussed so far may seem to go a long way towards creating a culture for diversity, but we have yet to begin on two key, interacting areas: organisational culture and the people who make it and carry it in their heads. A link between the 'hardware' and 'software' aspects of change can be forged by using the key questions below as a compass for progress made:

- Are people heard?
- Do people feel free to speak out against perceived wrong-doing?
- Are interpersonal problems fully explored?
- Are individuals recognised for their own strengths?
- Are people represented proportionately?
- Do all managers play an active part in creating and maintaining a culture for diversity?

Answering these questions honestly (possibly with the guidance of anonymous staff input) will indicate the level of change required and help to direct changes and training to develop people's self-awareness and behaviour.

Phase four – the 'software' side of organisational change

Nearly every attempt at organisational change has at its heart:

Changing what people 'think and do'.

The link between 'culture' and 'organisational success' is becoming better established and various studies now cite organisational culture as the most significant factor in ensuring success. Implicit in all organisational development initiatives, however, is the need to change people's attitudes, values, beliefs, basic assumptions and behaviour.

This means working on individual behaviour and also on how people think and behave across the entire organisation.

People cannot suddenly change a lifetime pattern of thinking and behaving overnight and the real issue of **how** we can reinvent the way we think and behave is often avoided in change management initiatives. It is this crucial element that we will address today.

People and performance

A study of manufacturing companies commissioned by the Institute of Personnel and Development (now the Chartered Institute of Personnel and Development) cited people management as critical to business performance and found its effects on the bottom line far exceeded those of an emphasis on quality, technology or competitive strategy. Yet managers seemed to concentrate on these issues and only half of the firms studied had a human resources manager, while few took a proactive approach to training. The authors concluded that the human relations climate has a big influence on performance and emphasised the importance of developing communities that involve and include everyone.

Source: 'Profitable personnel', by Michael West and Malcolm Patterson, *People Management*, 8 January 1998, pp28–31.

What are organisations?

Organisations are traditionally viewed as consisting of fairly tangible elements, such as:

- functions
- policies
- structures
- strategies.

But these are not really such solid areas as they sound. Originally, the word strategy, for example, was defined in military terms such as the art of planning war. This is inaccurate for today's organisations. It ignores important but less tangible notions, such as the individual, the group, autonomy and agency.

In addition, the limitations of the 'legacy of bureaucracy', mentioned on Sunday, are reinforced by:

- the historic roots of management in religious and military organisations

- the Industrial Revolution and its image of people as functional hands or cogs in a machine.

This all contributes to a mindset that plays down the human element that is so central to successful change management. Too often, we fail to deal with how people might fit into the change equation and neglect elements such as:

- *autonomy and free choice* – how we can all choose to go along with something for the sake of convenience or necessity, but not really believe in it or accept it
- *creativity and innovation* – how creativeness tends not to flourish in an environment that stifles individuality
- *the role of emotions* – how our feelings, such as anxiety or embarrassment, combined with our attitudes, values and beliefs, create a world that is not logical or rational.

The assumptions behind the mechanistic, rationalist view of organisational life have far-reaching consequences for change and development. They take no account of the intangible world that culture represents or of organisations as communities, with human considerations and problems.

As a result, there seems to be what might be described as a 'reality gap' between much modern management theory and strategy formulation and our ability to implement these. Strategies and policies that, theoretically, lay great stress on the value and importance of people often seem not to be fully realised in people's working lives. Excellent policies to deal with human issues, such as communications, discrimination or workplace bullying, seem sometimes to have little or no impact on day-to-day life. People then perceive them as more rhetoric than reality and lose trust in management.

Our approach to developing the 'software' side of a culture for diversity attempts to address this 'reality gap' through advanced forms of training aimed at helping us to:

- become more aware of our behaviour, our limitations and our impact on others
- appreciate our own part in bringing policies into practice.

Our cultural blindspots

In practice, culture affects how we think and behave and the decisions we make. We are not always rational, either as individuals or within our organisational context. We are usually biased in some ways, without being aware of it, and this element of cultural blindness will affect how we function in, for example, recognising new market opportunities or new ways of working. It can also affect how we view people from different groups.

To combat cultural blindness and develop a culture for diversity, the ability to think critically is crucial. The MDT approach aims to help us to critically review our past learning.

MDT – setting the foundations

Four areas of importance for MDT are:

1 a safe learning environment
2 a group context
3 feedback
4 highly specialised facilitation skills.

A safe learning environment
MDT depends first and foremost on creating a safe, supportive learning environment, with trust well established between trainer and participants.

A group context
The emphasis on group work stems from the social constructionist approach discussed on Wednesday, and is vital to the process of learning, through MDT, about our behaviour, blindspots and impact on others. It is especially helpful if those in a group are colleagues or peers and have significant relationships with one another.

Although our attitudes, values, beliefs and assumptions may seem very private, other people strongly influence them.

Feedback
Learning from others about behaviour or attitudes of which we are not aware is vital for our development. Most of us would be surprised about the effects and messages caused by some of our behaviours, and to develop a culture for diversity we need to learn to recognise and reduce our blindspots, at both the individual and organisational levels. MDT aims to create an environment within which people can give and receive honest, non-judgemental and descriptive feedback, with minimum threat to themselves or others.

Facilitation skills
The facilitator's role is central in developing and implementing MDT and supporting the giving or receiving of feedback. He or she requires personal awareness, knowledge about facilitation and group processes, listening skills, directness and honesty. Knowledge of how to use

aspects of existing culture to develop new learning is also important.

We all hope that we possess such qualities, but most will require training and personal development to facilitate MDT.

Summary

Today, we finished going through 'hardware' issues by looking at new processes or structures that could help people feel more included and contribute to a better approach to managing diversity. We began on phase four, the 'software' of change, looking once more at how our view of an organisation so easily neglects the people who form it. Then we started to lay the ground for MDT, discussing its four main elements of a safe learning environment, a group context for learning, sensitive feedback and skilled facilitation.

Tomorrow, we will conclude by outlining some relevant theories and techniques, and then go through the main buildings blocks for an MDT training programme.

Multi-Dimensional Training

For this last day of our week, the plan is to:

- look briefly at some background theories and techniques that will help us to understand the MDT approach
- go through the main elements of the training itself
- summarise the key issues emphasised in this approach to developing a culture for diversity.

Background theories and techniques

Cognitive dissonance
Cognitive dissonance is a feeling that can force us out of our 'comfort zone' and into the learning of new behaviours. Cognitive dissonance can come into operation if we act in a way that is negative without being aware of it – perhaps by behaving in a bullying way – and then find out from others' feedback how they perceived our behaviour.

This is likely to make us aware of an inconsistency between how we would like to be seen and how we are actually seen.

Johari's Window
Luft and Ingham's Johari's Window model shows how the giving and receiving of feedback on our behaviour and its effects can help us to achieve personal development.

As two columns, the four panes represent the 'self', while as two rows, they represent the 'group'. The information contained in the panes, rows and columns moves around from pane to pane, as the level of mutual trust and feedback vary within the group. Because of this movement, the size and shape of the panes will vary.

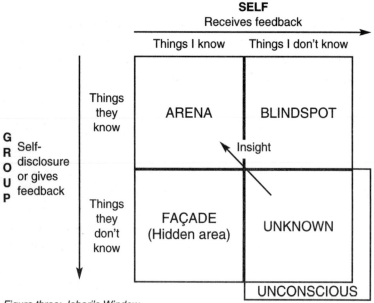

Figure three: Johari's Window

The **Arena pane** contains things known about the self by both self and group and should increase in size as trust develops and more personal information is shared.

The **Blindspot pane** contains information not known by the self but which the group might know of. Within a group, participants communicate all kinds of information of which they are not aware, but which others will pick up. Through their feedback, we can learn about:

• the verbal cues we use
• the opinions we exhibit

- our mannerisms
- our ways of saying things
- the style in which we relate to others.

The **Façade pane** represents things that we know but hide from others in the group because of fear of rejection or attack. This fear should recede as a safe learning environment becomes more established and supportive elements within the group are seen.

The **Unknown pane** contains things that neither we nor the group know about ourselves.

The process of giving and receiving feedback to decrease our blindspots will increase our awareness about ourselves. This will move the vertical line between the Johari's Window panes to the right as our unintentional tendencies to bias, prejudice and discrimination are lessened, as we find out more about ourselves.

Defence routines
We all seek to maintain a feeling of control that can require some distortion of our view of the external world and this may lead to behaviour that an outsider would find irrational. Both individuals and organisations develop defence routines to avoid anxiety. While we can never be fully aware of these, we can develop our ability to recognise them, particularly with the help of feedback from others.

Anxiety, possibly beginning in one person but seeming to spread to others, can lead to defensive or avoidance behaviours, such as:

- distancing a subject through intellectualising it
- avoiding recognition of negative feelings by blaming others.

We are rarely aware of when we are acting out our unconscious defence mechanisms, but others can help us to recognise and discuss this situation.

Organisational defence routines and flight behaviour
In organisations, defence routines can become institutionalised, blocking responsiveness and the capacity to implement change. For example, planned action for change might be indirectly procrastinated for no real reason through the forming of a committee, with long or limitless time to discuss and work on issues or objectives.

Creating a culture for diversity will almost inevitably involve challenging some strongly established defence routines. Understanding the largely subconscious processes involved will make it easier to intervene in a way that can motivate people to want to change, for their own reasons.

Groups and change – brief psychological background

1930s onwards – the Gestalt school
This is still influential in many respects. Gestaltist psychologists developed a theory of cognitive balance, suggesting that the more balanced our way of seeing things is, the harder it will be for us to change. This approach introduces a motivational aspect to individual change, in that we seem to dislike contradiction or uncertainty.

We prefer, for instance, to think of things in terms of good and bad, even though the world may not really be so simple. We also seem not to like it when our values or beliefs become challenged or muddled, and to have an inborn wish to return to our previous state of cognitive balance, however illogical we may know it to be.

J E Eiser has suggested that this sort of thinking leads to intolerance, prejudice and simplistic solutions, based on the elimination of uncertainty, mixture and opposition. His warning, however, is rarely recognised.

Early 1940s – Kurt Lewin
Lewin's wartime research, comparing ways of persuading people to change their dietary habits, led him to identify the importance of involving people in discussion about proposed change. Group discussions proved far more effective than a lecturing approach in attempts to bring about change.

1950s – E B Pelz
While investigating the reasons for the greater effectiveness of discussion in promoting change, Pelz found evidence of two important factors affecting the attitudes of the groups.

1 A new, shared group norm evolved during discussions and came into participants' awareness.
2 The free choice involved in the act of making a decision led to greater commitment in carrying out whatever choice was made.

The MDT training programme

Change is no easy matter. We have had to grapple with some hard theoretical ideas and issues in order to be able to grasp the underlying concepts. Now, we may understand how the barriers to a culture for diversity that exist in our ingrained attitudes, values and beliefs might be overcome with concentrated, well-supported training, such as a focused MDT programme. The effects of this on our learning capacity, together with continued programme support and evaluation to consolidate changes, can motivate us to reassess and possibly restructure our attitudes, values and beliefs.

Within the context of the theories discussed, and with a supporting analysis of the existing organisational culture and its rituals, myths, ceremonies and symbols, a training programme for change can be designed. This can be tailored to an organisation and will aim to help people develop more critical thinking power and see beyond some of their prejudices.

The design of a training programme of this sort is important, because most of us learn in a way that does not help us to reflect on, or analyse, our attitudes and behaviour in a critical way. The training needs to offer structured experiences introducing participants' actual attitudes and behaviours or 'theories in use'. As individuals and as a group, participants can then observe, evaluate, reflect upon and contrast the actual attitudes and behaviours enacted with their stated views and attitudes, or 'espoused theory'.

'Espoused theories' and 'theories in use' are concepts introduced by Chris Argyris and Donald A Schon in their seminal book on organisational culture and learning, *Organisational Learning: Theory, method and practice* (2nd edn, Reading, Mass., Addison Wesley, 1996). They are a way of describing the fact that most of us do not always 'practice what we preach' and often act in ways that contradict our supposed values and ideas, without necessarily realising it.

Simply understanding that different attitudes and behaviour are a good idea will not usually help us to change in the long term. For this, people need to experience behaving in a different way during training and they are then more likely to behave differently in the workplace. MDT involves designing experiences that offer such opportunities in the form of case studies, combined with experiential learning.

The building blocks for MDT

The role of rituals, ceremonies, drama and symbols
By identifying rituals, ceremonies, drama or symbols that are important to people in the organisation, it becomes possible to use these to motivate people to listen to what we say with more interest.

Rituals are an important part of culture, especially in hierarchical organisations. They impart meaning and values through the ways in which things are done, while the 'content' of what is done – the actual action or discussion involved – may easily become lost or distorted. Rituals can be understood as encoded forms of communication of, for example, people's status or acceptability within the organisation, or expectations for responses or behaviours. We are not normally aware of their existence or significance, but they nevertheless communicate much to us through how things happen and can be recognised and decoded by an objective observer.

When we are party to an organisational ritual we do not normally recognise it ourselves. Yet if the ritual were to change from the established way of doing things, then we would be likely to know at once that something was wrong.

Using rituals to support learning

Multi-Dimensional Training was used in a public sector service organisation to develop a culture within which people could learn to trust in grievance procedures, though they had traditionally viewed the use of these as a form of 'career suicide'. The 334 managers participating in the training programme were largely hostile to the change process.

To help managers see the relevance of the issues involved, a test ritual known to be used at the start of their service training was built into the MDT programme. This was a knowledge test, based on a booklet sent out before the training started. The test was given, then scored, at the opening of the course. The aim was not to evaluate knowledge, but to use a simple, familiar ritual (the test) to involve participants in the learning process.

Observation and later interviews affirmed that the test had gained people's attention. One comment captures this point:

'*Travelling to the course on the first day, everybody was making derogatory remarks about the course and grievances. Travelling to the course on the second day people were talking about the grievance procedure and things that had happened.*'

The rituals, symbols and drama through which culture is learned and sustained can help us to change culture, if used in a consistent way. The example above built on participants' high valuation of concrete facts and knowledge, as opposed to the people-related issues that they considered 'soft' and 'woolly', abstract concepts. It helped to engage them in the learning process, after which it was easier for participants to choose to move on to less concrete areas, such as aspects of discrimination and the process of dealing with grievances.

Case studies
Real case studies, based on experiences and events within the organisation, can be created during the early stages of a change programme, although real names and positions should be disguised. The case studies should be distributed during a Multi-Dimensional Training event and used as an individual or small group exercise to:

- act as a vehicle to examine 'theories in use' and defence routines in the organisation
- identify barriers to change in the organisation
- help to identify likely negative consequences of attitudes or behaviour.

Afterwards, a full group debrief and discussion can focus upon examining what happened and the possible effects of particular courses of action. This allows participants to voice their opinions and state what they would do and how they would do it.

Such exercises should reveal contrasts between people's espoused theories and their active 'theories in use'. But the knowledge and understanding gained from this contrast represents only part of the learning process. If the training is ended at this point, little real or lasting change is likely to result in practice.

Simulation or structured experience
To move beyond this stage, people need to actively experience changing attitudes and behaviour and simulations or structured experiences can help them achieve this. Through simulation, learning is reinforced by experience, allowing participants to build a clear picture of how their new behaviour looks and the effects it may have.

Within a safe learning environment, simulations based on real experiences in the organisation can be used to enable individuals to reappraise their freely chosen attitudes and behaviour. This reappraisal takes place with the help of others, who are able to give their views on negative consequences of the attitudes or behaviour enacted. The simulations should:

- be designed to target areas of culture that threaten the successful implementation of a culture of diversity
- present a real and unexpected dilemma to participants
- be enacted without any guidance from the facilitator about possible responses.

The aim is to set a scene within which participants have total freedom to decide how to respond. Afterwards, they can identify possible negative consequences following from their freely chosen behaviour, with the help of effective debriefing and group feedback.

This process gives a base of concrete experience for exploring the complexities within difficult situations. It helps to change people's mental representations of action and consolidates their learning experience more effectively than is possible through understanding alone.

For example, someone with an espoused theory of 'valuing diversity' may be asked to take part in a simulation of dealing with a poorly performing member of staff who is from a minority group. This will give the opportunity to check out the consistency between his or her espoused theory and theory in use. Feedback from 'significant others' – peers, subordinates and superiors – will highlight 'blindspot' areas, for example giving an impression of not listening to what the person says or showing a stereotyping attitude in some way that they are unaware of.

Feedback concerning the likely negative consequences of our attitudes and behaviour can lead to real attitude change that will carry forward into our lives. If participants can also, directly or vicariously, experience behaviour that will have more positive consequences, then their behaviour beyond the training room is likely to develop and change as well.

Job simulations can create particular enthusiasm and develop a sense of togetherness through the enacting of the same difficult, but exciting, experience. Managers of all levels can play different roles. A director, for example, can play the role of a supervisor, or a supervisor the role of a general manager. In this way, people can come to a better understanding of the perspectives and problems relating to different organisational levels.

There are many possible simulations that can be created to expose both the positive and the negative aspects of an organisation's culture, so that people:

- can see and understand situations more fully for themselves
- can therefore go on to challenge aspects of their organisation's culture, as their beliefs change.

Debriefing
Effective debriefing is a vital part of MDT. All participants will have achieved either direct or vicarious experience that provides an in-depth learning experience. The debriefing process can, for example, involve an agreement within a group of senior managers concerning suitable attitudes and

behaviour within the organisation. If so, these views are likely to become extremely powerful and will act to change the culture.

The element of free choice, however, is essential. Without full realisation of the problems inherent in their own behaviour or attitudes, participants will not be able to, and may not understand the need for, change. Rather than pointing out any problem areas identified, the facilitator or facilitators should provide careful guidance to help participants themselves to recognise aspects of behaviour that could have positive or negative consequences. The facilitation should be as supportive as possible and participants should be encouraged to contribute during these sessions.

The debriefing of simulations or structured experiences seems to:

- have the power to provide participants with a model on which they can base future action
- give participants the confidence to deal with situations in a new way
- let participants know that they have the support of others who have experienced the training with them.

During debriefs, possible strategies are sometimes developed on how to deal with a range of situations and, most importantly, these are developed by the participants, on the basis of their own newly acquired knowledge and experience.

Over this week, we have attempted to understand how it is possible to create a culture for diversity. In practice, of course, this process will take much longer than a week and will require sustained support and commitment from everyone, especially leaders within the organisation.

Conclusion

Throughout this week, we have looked at:

- what diversity is, and how our social and work context is changing in ways that require a constructive management response
- the importance of an open culture as a platform for greater diversity
- the effects of our failure to manage diversity on some particular groups
- how easily our understanding of organisations is still shaped by history rather than present knowledge
- how individual and cultural change can be achieved through focusing on the 'hardware' of change (structures, systems and processes) and the 'software' of change (people and culture)
- the theories, techniques, concepts and buildings blocks of the MDT training approach to helping us learn more about ourselves – and possibly change as a consequence.

All attempts to change an organisation, including the attempt to create a culture for diversity, centre on changing what people do and how they think. This means changing people's attitudes and behaviour and such changes cannot be achieved through structural changes or processes alone.

To create a culture for diversity, it is important to develop higher levels of self-awareness and critical thinking among managers in an organisation. We have to be aware of:

- how culture affects how we think and behave
- how our behaviour affects others
- how others' behaviour affects us
- the existence of our own biases and prejudices
- our feelings and emotions and their effects on our behaviour and decisions
- feelings and emotions in others and how we may respond to them.

To achieve such high levels of awareness, some key skills are essential, including:

- critical thinking
- skilled observation
- seeing beyond the obvious
- empathy.

To use such skills while experiencing the heat and happenings of reality requires the key quality of self-control, together with the ability to recognise and reflect upon our attitudes, values and beliefs and evaluate their relevance for today.

Multi-Dimensional Training is an effective way of developing these skills and qualities. It is basically focused on developing personal and interpersonal skills and therefore involves emotions as well as knowledge. When used within organisations, MDT has been found to be a powerful motivator for change, resulting in strong, measurable and lasting changes in people's attitudes and behaviour.

The Multi-Dimensional Training approach requires senior management involvement, commitment and willingness to lead changes from the front. It is relevant for many change contexts, but is especially applicable in developing a culture for diversity, which requires high levels of self and behavioural awareness from everyone, especially leaders and managers.